Where I'd Watch Plastic Trees Not Grow

Hannah Hodgson

VERVE
POETRY PRESS
BIRMINGHAM

PUBLISHED BY VERVE POETRY PRESS
https://vervepoetrypress.com
mail@vervepoetrypress.com

FIRST PUBLISHED FEB 2021

Printed and bound in the UK
by Positive Print, Birmingham

ISBN: 978-1-912565-53-5

CONTENTS

Acknowledgements

To Mum – for putting up with my messy room and messy life. All my love, Hannah xx

Where I'd Watch Plastic Trees Not Grow

The Orchard

The trees here grow medical conditions.
I'm second from the left, and each fruit is a crystallised diagnosis.

They're quite remarkable - have a snap like pea pods
and a taste you can't really ground. I'm biblical,

in that once you pick a fruit, regret
isn't enough to make it reattach.

Feel free to have a look around. I'd walk quickly though,
you don't want to be here when they land.

Long-Term Illness

After Time Machine *by Nick Drake*

Over 200 cars crashed in the fog,
one into another, into another.
I was in the first car, the engine spluttering,

unravelling in the road –
and others couldn't help but join in.
Some bullseyed their windscreens,

languished on their bonnets with me –
while others politely nudged their car
into the next, just wanting to be part of the tragedy.

I was the only fatality, and after the initial shock
they left – their cars reverse blooming, rewinding
down the carriageway without me.

Isolation Ward

The air was supposed to be filtered
but I knew it was a Tuesday by the smell of chips
wafting through the vents into my hospital room.

The windows held two atmospheres centimetres apart,
protected me like wary parents from the uncontrollable.
They didn't open – contained me indoors

as if I were a monkey, almost human.
They were supposed to be airtight
but once a spider broke in,

found a glitch in the medical world,
squeezed under the silicone.
A nurse squashed him with a library book

before I could stop her, before I could marvel
something I hadn't seen for six months.
The doctors were supposed to diagnose,

to know for certain, but I found my diagnosis
on Google – knew the answer
before the arrival of my test results.

The tree in outpatients was plastic, and every night I'd watch it not grow from my window

In those six months,
the ward became a garden –

relatives sat in daisy chains
around sick children's beds.

Most days, I followed fairy steps
along to the pond which the nurses

had covered using a grate.
There was a field of wildflowers

which grew at the same rate
as hair follicles from my bald patch.

Once, I stumbled upon a parliament of crows
who were soon to begin a post- mortem.

Eventually, doctors felt my body
had earned the key to its own front garden.

Before leaving, I threw everything
on a bonfire the kids from renal were using

to roast marshmallows. My mum
laid out her belongings into two piles

brought home: three t-shirts and a singular photo
I keep on the mantelpiece of my chest as a threat

to the body, a reminder of where we'll go back to.

Dear Visitors

I've become a tiger, and this ward is a zoo.
Pay your entrance fees at the nurse's station,

and gawp as you arrive at my cubicle.
Showtimes are twice daily for an hour.

Things don't end well for those who linger.
Don't maudle, as the captive here that's my job.

Ask and answer questions. Reveal a little
of your flesh, trust I won't rip you apart.

Talk of the wild, talk of home.
Meet me at midnight with the bolt cutters.

In the Half-light

after Carole Bromley

The sign is reassuring
like a piece of hardened skin rubbed subconsciously.
    You are in Salford Royal Hospital,
    the Ladywell unit, ward H8

The ward has low rumblings of pain.
A withdrawing alcoholic
the staff have hidden the hand gel from.
A missing curtain thanks to a splatter of blood.
The air is restless with forced proximity,
polite unbearability.

When the nurse goes to the bathroom,
a patient stands on the medicine cabinet
to open a window. Her silhouette
an expectant mother, her body
pre-empting liver failure.

Crashing

Every 200 yards there's a telephone in the hospital.
The only emergency number a single 9, and a crash call is sent to all pagers.

Doctors descend on the scene, purposeful. Their determined faces
could startle any heart back into sinus rhythm.

The crash trolley is rushed down the corridor – adrenaline drawn
from the air and injected in seconds. A defibrillator is attached to the chest

and decisions are made within the hour. I've seen my consultant cry once.
When she couldn't save a life, deserted by her superpower.

Death Rattle

Back in the day, everyone loved a good hanging –
curiosity gathered in the town square, red-nosed,
waiting for the theatre of mortality to end.

Today I attract the equivalent crowd –
have to untangle my vocal cords
from intrusive questioning.

Hospice is an experience with the brink,
as near the cliff edge you can go without falling.
Natural death isn't quick.

It begins with a storm brewing in the chest –
thunder of increasing intensity,
crackles of lightning in the airway.

It ends with a moment of clarity,
final words like an April shower
slowly evaporating.

After the Curtain

We aren't allowed to draw the curtains
that surround our beds. Nurses need to count us.
Our bodies make us inmates.

Today we are silent, each of us willing our breath sounds
to be coming from her mouth.
The woman in the next bed doesn't wake up.

This isn't an episode of ER
where I begin a dramatic monologue
and the SATs monitor begins to record.

Her children arrive, her daughter crying neatly
in the corner. Her husband stands
spinning his wedding band around his finger.

They leave as the Porters enter
with a dull steel gurney, and a body bag.
A nurse remembers paperwork,

turns back towards the office,
collects this bureaucracy the dead don't care for.
My chest heaves as a nurse closes my curtain,

spares me from watching the inerasable.
The Porters strain as they transfer her,
the industrial plastic crinkling

as the bag is zipped up. It takes three attempts
for the trolley to fit back into the corridor,
after each failure the Porters murmur.

A nurse fills carrier bags marked 'patient property',
while another opens my curtained barrier.
The bedding is changed, surfaces wiped down,

the bed space marked *vacant*
on the computer system.

A&E, England, Jan 2020

He was on a trolley in the corridor,
as his body began hardening slowly,
setting like air dried plaster.

There were two car accidents,
three heart attacks and a miscarriage –
and his outcome had been inevitable.

He lay there for four hours
while the waiting room stared on,
staff unable to move him –
his death a macabre art installation.

Leaflet dispensed by crows who circle around the resus bay like overstated authority figures

People with Cardiac conditions often experience
a sense of impending doom.
It's the hearts call
to the brain for Marshall law.

Each cell is a police officer
clad in riot gear,
deployed to essential functions –
the brain, lungs and vascular system.

Possible causes include:
a blackout, an arrhythmia or panic attack.
As the Prime Minister of your body, remain calm –
pretend everything will be fine (even though it won't).

Bad News

Doctors transform into poets as they deliver bad news.
>*Declining/*
>*another step in the wrong direction/*
>*no more invasive tests/*
>*sick enough to die/*

A flower waiting in a vase,
or a wick burning too quickly.
They reposition the tissue box, crack a joke
before dismantling my world.
There's no easy way to say this.

Grandad

Meet me at yours, ten years before.
Let the cigarette you accidentally burned me with be your last.
Trap doors appear when you least expect them;
 and yours swallowed you whole.
I wish I could peel back the corner of my door
like wrapping paper, and check you're there
before my body decides to jump.

Little Deaths

After the death of my stomach,
the church was full of mourners –

but at the 15th funeral of myself
it's just me and a few doctors.

We lay wreathes by each ear
and seal each urn with a hearing aid mould.

I'm a widower grieving herself.
My stem still living,

while all the petals have died;
my body has begun to droop.

The only person I knew with my condition

is dead. Her mother posted the news on Facebook
to over a thousand comments –
platitudes that land like butterflies
hardened mid-flight. Some hijack the tragedy,
metamorphosize into water features,
enjoy the act of sobbing with reason.
The hospice adds her name
to the roll call of the dead;
wooden hearts which hang
above the nurses station,
the opposite of a baby's mobile.

10th April 2020

Dad has mowed the lawn two days in a row.
It explains our lives now – the pushing along

of a machine, blades with nothing to cut –
acting our lives out just to be purposeful.

I got dressed up for a zoom conference
and cried at a kind letter which landed on the doormat.

I need two witnesses who aren't beneficiaries
to finalise my will. My lawyer suggests

I ask my neighbours to watch through the window,
because even with expected deaths the Government

aren't changing the rules. The GP rang this afternoon
trying to talk about a DNR order. I refused,

instead told him about starlings murmurating
and all the living I have left to do.

52nd Day of Self Isolation

It has been the sort of day
in which I learned slugs have holes
which parasites live in.

The day you reserve
the special biscuits for, and watch
a unique kind of rubbish on Netflix.

It's transforming into that sort of week.
Where the days drag like a foot
and the leather of your shoe is ruptured.

The kind you can't really describe
and if someone asks you say you're fine.
It's worse than neutral
but not terrible enough to be memorable.

My Mother's Russian Dolls

were hand painted, had sun faded backs
from their brief years on my windowsill.

They had soft faces, the type of smile
a quietly seething mum would have.

There were three of them, but the tiny doll
inside the third one is missing –

the last in a generation of matriarchs
unable to fulfil her purpose.

There is an Art to Falling

after Kim Moore

Carpet is preferable, a cushioned landing on the cheap –
avoid the wrists. Learn not to save yourself.
Fall as you would bellyflop into a pool
fall as you would into raked leaves in the garden.

Release. Trust the body knows what it's doing.
Try landing on your knees,
or better, sit down, as I did in a supermarket.
Drink water – if you can,

eat something – if you can,
reignite the furnace of your body,
blow on its embers.
Assess every room for its safety,

its sharp corners – your body
soon to be a separate entity.
Ask somebody to raise your legs
feet together, reverse praying.

Be grateful for the days
a faint doesn't drag with its weighted cloak,
to visit a night sky with no stars.

The Rainbow Room

After Rebecca Goss

This isn't the room you're told bad news in.
It's the one you're taken to once you know it.

It has green polyester carpets, framed landscapes, soundproof walls
and a single shelf filled with waiting, empty memory books.

There are two tall glass doors covered by Venetian blinds in the corner.
We are never told what was behind them, but as sick kids

we know; more comfortable with death than adults.
The room has a heavy quiet – she and I slipped in three years ago,

to paint our nails away from the thrum of the sensory room.
Today, her mother sits on the same beige sofa,

waiting to see her daughter – fresh faced and inanimate –
on a cooled mattress.

Everybody Loves a Dying Girl

After Tishani Doshi

Some girls avoid me in town,
cross the road to avoid
maudlin' contagion.
While others come over to chat –

gather pieces of information
they scrunch, and throw
onto the bonfire of prattle.
At parties I'm everyone's friend,

I travel in their mouths,
discussed, even though
I'm not there. Gossip
swirling in drinks like mixers.

I wish for the truth –
to hear what they say
without their masks on,
without their filters activated

by my sitting feet away.
I wish to reject my sainthood –
illness doesn't cure me of a personality,
of doing things which are unforgivable.

We the Grieving

If people were lightbulbs, they would cast off their glass shell
and reveal their filament for my inspection.
>   *My wife had bowel cancer; our friends stopped coming over.*
>   *After she died, they never came back.*

Our experiences differ, but could be bundled together as postcards
in a junk shop. We are a people who know the definition of Terrible.
Terrible is a room without a door, it leeches colour,
damaging all which should be untouchable.
We have a fear of attachment thanks to the Terrible,
enclose ourselves like caterpillars
waiting for the day our bodies transform.

Decompose with me

After Carol Ann Duffy's Small Female Skull

Learn all my heart truly knows,
its four chambers
thickened with the velvet of diet.

Study my kidneys
as they begin to dry out –
two halves of a tomato.

Watch my capillaries
as they burst their banks;
the stain creeping
along my skin
like a tablecloth.

Count the inches
as my hair continues
to grow, as the rest of me
begins a disappearing act.

Watch, I melt
into the earth like butter.

ACKNOWLEDGEMENTS

To Mum and Dad, thank you for your empathy, practical thinking and hard work.

Poetry is lifesaving. Not just the words but the people behind them. These poems wouldn't have come to exist without Kim Moore, my friend and mentor. We met at Dove Cottage Young Poets, funded by The Wordsworth Trust. My sincere thanks to them.

Thanks also to my Friday poetry feedback group. You've taught me many things about my work, as well as humour in all its forms.

Essential thanks go to my NHS team. Dr Paine, Dr Fitchett, Dave Howard, Dr Roberts, Dr Sayer and the Palliative medicine team, as well as St Mary's Hospice and staff at the Mark Holland Trust. Thanks will never be enough.

Thanks to the Writing Squad, especially Steve Dearden for his quiet and essential work of putting writers first. Inside the Squad I've been mentored by Malika Booker; whose precise feedback was very helpful. Thanks also to members of the Poets Minigoals group, who kept me alive during a very dark time last year.

To my good friend Lydia Allison, I didn't really know you before the pandemic, but the hours we've spent talking have been a joy. Thanks also to Jessica Wood and Laura Potts, for lovely poetic and spiritual catchups.

Finally, my thanks to the Society of Authors, whose emergency grant meant I could purchase accessible equipment and finish this manuscript; and to The Northern Writers Awards, specifically Will Mackie and Vahni Capildeo, for their encouragement and financial support.

ABOUT THE AUTHOR:

Hannah Hodgson is a poet living with life limiting illness. Her work has been published by the Poetry Society, Teen Vogue and Poetry Salzburg, amongst others. She is a recipient of a 2020 Northern Writers Award for Poetry. Her first poetry pamphlet *Dear Body* was published by Wayleave Press in 2018.

ABOUT VERVE POETRY PRESS

Verve Poetry Press is a quite new and already award-winning press that focused initially on meeting a local need in Birmingham - a need for the vibrant poetry scene here in Brum to find a way to present itself to the poetry world via publication. Co-founded by Stuart Bartholomew and Amerah Saleh, it now publishes poets from all corners of the UK and beyond - poets that speak to the city's varied and energetic qualities and will contribute to its many poetic stories.

Added to this is a colourful pamphlet series, many featuring poets who have performed at our sister festival - and a poetry show series which captures the magic of longer poetry performance pieces by festival alumni such as Polarbear, Matt Abbott and Geraldine Carver.

In 2019 the press was voted Most Innovative Publisher at the Saboteur Awards, and won the Publisher's Award for Poetry Pamphlets at the Michael Marks Awards.

Like the festival, we strive to think about poetry in inclusive ways and embrace the multiplicity of approaches towards this glorious art.

www.vervepoetrypress.com
@VervePoetryPres
mail@vervepoetrypress.com